Spiritual Care

A Practical Handbook

Rev. Moe Anderson

Copyright © 2014 by Rev. Moe Anderson

Spiritual Care
A Practical Handbook
by Rev. Moe Anderson

Printed in the United States of America

ISBN 9781628714920

All rights reserved solely by the author. The author guarantees all contents are original and do not infringe upon the legal rights of any other person or work. No part of this book may be reproduced in any form without the permission of the author. The views expressed in this book are not necessarily those of the publisher.

www.xulonpress.com

For Carolyn

Acknowledgements

It is with deepest gratitude that I say thank you to my family who has always been a source of encouragement to me and especially to the wonderful, young woman that I am so blessed to have as my daughter, Carolyn.

I am grateful for the many people throughout my career who served with me as teachers and mentors, volunteers and community clergy. Each one of you holds a special place in my heart.

It is with deepest honour I say thanks to the patients, residents and families who have allowed me to walk beside them through some of their most difficult times.

I would like to say a very special thanks to Max Ryan who was the gift of grace at just the right moment and provided countless hours of encouragement and editing. He and his wife Patricia have become soul friends in my journey.

Finally, I would like to say thank you to the team of Spiritual Care Professionals at The University Health Network and the staff of the Critical Care Program who have given me wings to fly. Each day that I have to work with you is a grace-filled gift.

Table of Contents

Chapter 1	Introduction – Spiritual Care Revisited	11
Chapter 2	Don't Forget the Dementia Patients	25
Chapter 3	Palliative and Dying for Spiritual Care	39
Chapter 4	Mental Health Issues	55
Chapter 5	Hospital Visits	61
Chapter 6	Residential Facilities	75
Chapter 7	Responding to Trauma	87
Chapter 8	Dealing With Disabilities	107
Chapter 9	Prayers and Readings	125

Chapter 1

Introduction

If you had told me when at age sixteen I was going to be a Spiritual Care Professional in the Critical Care Program of a large hospital, I would have laughed at you. At the time, a friend had been diagnosed with leukemia and visiting her in hospital was agonizing. The sights and smells of the hospital left me panicked and hearing people in pain in tears. In my twenties I found myself in a difficult situation. My husband was hit by a van while driving his bicycle, leaving him in the intensive care unit. My mother, diagnosed with cancer, was in another hospital in another city and my grandmother with end stage liver failure was in yet another hospital and city.

It was during this time, when family support was stretched, that I overcame my fear of hospitals. It is that time that I look back and am reminded of how God equips and helps us to grow spiritually.

As a lay person who visited people in the hospital, I realized that I was called to do this professionally and full-time. I went to seminary where I obtained a Master of Divinity and a Diploma in Spirituality in Healthcare. Over the years, I've done trauma training, non-violent crisis intervention, care for dementia population, Therapeutic Touch and Spiritual Direction. Each component added new ideas and ways of being with and helping people. I have a passion for visiting people who are in crisis and in hospital as well as a love of visiting people at all stages of their lives.

For several years, I have led workshops in conducting spiritual care and visiting for different faith traditions, denominations and groups. There are helpful brochures and pamphlets, though many are outdated and fail to capture the essence of spiritual care.

Introduction

Most books suggest that a visitor should call ahead and make an appointment, arrive at the appointed time, have a face to face conversation and then have a deep and theologically meaningful conversation. Most books suggest that you turn off distractions such as TV and radio to allow for conversation. This sounds like a good idea but you wouldn't be popular at our house if you turned off our favourite TV shows. You would, however, be welcome to watch it with us.

What about those who need a visit but can't hear a conversation or remember an appointment that you set? What about people who wouldn't feel comfortable with a face-to-face conversation?

Are there more efficient ways of communicating? It is my hope that this book will give food for thought, and help congregations identify where spiritual care is needed, how to do it effectively and how to find meaning and joy in spiritual care.

Why Do Spiritual Care and Visiting?

I am not going to suggest a theological reason and rationale for spiritual care and visiting. Please put this book down and find some other ministry if you need this. (If your motivation is to visit "the least of these," also put this book down. My patients and residents are not the "least of these.") They are people filled with a lifetime of stories of faith. Their ability to face their fears and sorrows and share these with someone is courageous.

I admire the young man who volunteered for me in spiritual care who suffers from an aggressive, debilitating condition. He is not stable enough to walk around the hospital but his organizational skills help to keep everyone else reminded of their responsibilities. Once in a while we meet to ensure we are on the same page. His courage, passion and enthusiasm inspire me.

At the long-term care facility where I worked, there is a team of residents who form "The Welcoming Committee." After they processed the pain of their own transitions into long-term care, they try to be on the scene early to help new residents to offer reassurance and advice on how to make the transition easier. They also offer reassurance to the families. They are open about how miserable they felt (and how difficult they were with their families) but they have found peace and joy and they still have bad days. There is no better testimony than their words and lives. Throughout this book you will find little vignettes of moments when God's light shone through my experiences of visiting and some of the ways that people's stories touched my life. I share them because I want you to think of visiting and spiritual care as a treasure hunt and an adventure.

The Changing Landscape of Care

Churches are aging faster than other volunteer and membership based organizations. While some would think this statistic as a negative, there is a silver lining (pun intended) in this cloud. It is that the church once again has the opportunity to lead the way in this culture by caring for and ministering to seniors. If you listen to the stories of how the residents survived the Great Depression, survived as single parents and widows during war times, saw one out of every 100 of their fellow Canadians die during WWII and subsequently survive through one of the worst pandemics that the world has ever seen, we actually have the greatest repository of information of how to care for many people with only a few within the walls of your church. People from that era have strong memories of being bombed, watching people go off to war, parents returning after years and meeting a four year old for the first time. Resources were scarce. It sometimes takes a little prodding but the there is a treasure trove of stories of survival and part of those stories of survival, are stories of faith.

This shift in the way illness, accidents and chronic conditions affects us, means that we must fundamentally shift the way we think of spiritual care. In the past, when sudden illness came, most people recovered or died within a relatively short period of time. There was more family around, neighbourhoods were more integrated and the survival period for the crisis was significantly shorter as we didn't have the medical technology. Churches could gear up their "casserole patrols" to bring meals to families for a short time. Working together as communities we could relatively easily assist a family in crisis with child-care, household tasks, rides, nursing assistance and all of the other tasks that become so onerous to a family in crisis. In many cases churches provided short-term financial assistance to those who were struggling.

Consider what is happening today. When a crisis hits the church gears up for a few weeks or months with casseroles, support, visits. The person who is so ill makes every effort to come to church, cheered on by a team of prayer warriors and enthusiastic supporters. They often receive medical treatment that will extend their life but limit their energy to participate in the life of the church. Their contribution to the home gradually diminishes with family and friends bearing the increasing burden. Over time, the ability for the family to participate in the life of the church gradually diminishes as their fatigue increases. A few faithful members will continue to visit until they move, die or go into retirement and nursing homes themselves.

If the average stay of a minister is 5-7 years, then there will be 2-4 ministers called to the church during the course of their illness. If the family is not attending and the minister is not active in visitation, forming a bond with a new person becomes increasingly difficult with each new transition. Many families that I meet talk about this pattern of the relationship to their church. This is not intentional on the part of the church. What has to be intentional is our plan to reach out to all members and maintain support and contact with them through visitation.

Look at your current church directory. How many people are listed who haven't been seen recently? Find a directory that is at least one year old, then five years. Many of the people who were dropped from one directory to the next never moved out of the area and most people can't identify a discernable reason for their departure. Had we hung on to everyone who disappeared from our directories in the last ten years, most churches would be double in size.

Mass Assessment

I work with large groups of people so how do you figure out who needs spiritual care the most on any given day? Sometimes it obvious by the tears in their eyes when they see you at church or the events that you know about. People are often struggling and could use the benefit of spiritual care. The signs are more subtle.

There are several ways that we can do mass assessments. The first is right before your eyes – who is or isn't in your congregation this Sunday? Working in long-term care, I'm required to take attendance to prove to the government that I am providing for the spiritual care needs of my residents. If residents aren't in attendance, I am required to document why they are not, noting whether they are sick, engaged in other programs, feeling depressed, are engaged in an independent leisure activity or have just said no to the invitation. I am required to demonstrate that I have made church as accessible as possible for all my residents by providing one-to-one support if needed, transportation to service, realigning their baths, showers and medication schedules with nursing so as not to interfere with their attendance and ensure that recreation doesn't provide programs that compete with church. Large print for all handouts, hearing assistance and seating all make a difference. For one person, it was as simple as handing him the newspaper each time he came to wait for a service that encouraged him to stay and participate. I often tease local clergy that they should have a house key and a bus that they drive around to ensure that they get all of their parishioners to Sunday service! Can you imagine arriving in the homes of everyone and removing all of the barriers it takes to get them to church! Talk to the baseball coach to reschedule games, speak with their friends if they are hosting dinner parties that are making them too tired to participate, pick them up if their car has broken down. You could even open their wallets and plunk in their tithe! I know it sounds silly but if you consider that visitation is built on the cornerstone of communities that maximize the opportunity for everyone to participate, how often do we ask what are the barriers preventing people from coming to church. Once I have accounted for their attendance in programs, it is my responsibility to ensure that I am providing them with programs that are of interest. If they are not participating, I must document that I am meeting their spiritual needs and what the plan is to meet those needs.

If you want an interesting exercise, sit down with your church directory after your next church service and account for everyone on that list. If they were there, mark them present. If they were hospitalized or institutionalized, mark that down. If they have kids in sports or are travelling, make a notation. Those who you can't account for, make it a project to find out why. Some may have decided to sleep in. That's OK, the Psalmist says, "God grants sleep to those he loves." Bless them in their experience of

God's love. Some may have chosen to go golfing. (I'd rather be golfing than listening to my own sermon.) Sometimes God speaks more loudly in creation than through me. This exercise is not a witch hunt for wayward heathen but a prayerful attempt to discern the genuine needs of the congregation for spiritual care and visitation.

The second way to do mass assessment is to utilize the technology available to us and send out a mass e-mail. Next time you are reading through a book and find a poem, passage or reflection that touches you, send it to your entire congregation. I personally refrain from sending jokes or forwarding e-mails that come to me but look for more obscure items that will give a moment of reflection. By their response, members of the congregation will indicate if they are struggling.

Prayer is the language of mass assessment that we have forgotten. We often sit down with a list of people we think we should visit but rarely spend a moment (and I do mean just one) in quiet reflection and prayer and ask God who we are suppose to visit today? Where should we be today?

Visitation through Technology

I think of Jesus rowing away from the crowd on boat and wonder what would have happened if Jesus had been born during this technology age. We have multiple ways for people to access us. There is phone, pager, e-mail addresses, Skype, Facebook, cell-phones, MSN. These are all the ways that we can be reached. How many of them are you using to reach people? Invite everyone in an e-mail to send you their prayer requests and visit with them in your prayers.

Another tool that we can use for mass assessment is to be intentional about attendance at church. Don't just count the number of people who are there but actually mark down who was there and who was not. Were they enjoying a vacation or were they in trouble this week? Done correctly, attendance says that your participation in the community is important and if the circumstances prevent you from coming to us then we will come to you. It is not punitive but one way that we assess people who need follow-up support. We discover problems and issues before they become bigger than they need to be.

Chapter 2

Don't Forget
the Dementia Patients

In just about every congregation, one of the largest groups of people who we should be visiting are those suffering from some form of dementia. Many people are tempted to not visit them because they think that the patient won't remember the visit.

First of all, people who suffer from dementia experience it to varying degrees on different days. One day a person may not remember you but then the next time they greet you by name and treat you like a long-lost friend. Secondly, they certainly won't remember you if you don't visit them often. Have you ever met someone who greeted you by name but you couldn't remember theirs?

Why was that? It was because you didn't see them often enough to remember their name, especially if they were out of context. It is no different than those suffering from dementia who have an even smaller repository of memory to draw on. What is important to the care of dementia patients is that, as much as possible, the same people should visit them for continuity of care. Ideally, if there are those within the church who knew them prior to the development of dementia, this will help as earlier memories are sometimes more accessible. Regardless of whether or not they remember you or your visit, the visit is meaningful in the moment for that resident and forever for their families. Whatever delights your presence brought them, whatever comfort that you gave them is valued at the time. If there is no one in the congregation that knows the person, by all means visit them and make a new friend.

Challenges in Visitation

We always have the same conversation or they always ask me the same questions!

The first thing you need to remember is that they are not asking you the same questions or telling you the same information because they are trying to annoy you. They truly don't remember the answers you have already given them or the information that you have shared. One of the ways that I deal with this is to find a different response or answer to their questions every time. This keeps my mind working and often, a different response will elicit a different conversation even from residents with advanced dementia. For instance, what if a resident repeatedly asks if you have ever been to Windsor? You can either repeatedly answer yes or no to the question or try one of these responses:

I never have, what do you like about Windsor?
I know that there is a large automotive sector there.

Did you live there as a child? (Earlier memories are usually easier for patients suffering from dementia to recall).

That is the worst city for _____.

That is the best city for _____.

Who do you know from Windsor?

When was the last time that you visited?

For many types of dementia, memories are erased from most recent, backwards so any way you can ask questions or talk about things that would have been in their earlier memories, normally allows the resident to harness the greatest repository of memories in their storehouse. For instance, I might say something like,

Did they bring the milk on horse-drawn carriages in Windsor too?

Did your mother threaten to sell you to the shinny man?

I had never hear of "the shinny man" until we were talking about phrases of the Great Depression one day in Bible study and one resident talked about her mother threatening to sell her to the shinny man when she was misbehaving. The residents laughed. They knew that the shinny man was the Great Depression's travelling version of a yard sale. Families who were on the brink of financial collapse would sell even their most valuable possessions for a few pennies in order to feed their families. I had never heard this phrase before but when I saw their eyes light up in recognition, I began to ask residents in my locked dementia units and sure enough it was a trigger phrase for them as well. It was a phrase that got them talking and remembering.

The shinny man also became a great spiritual concept to talk about. The shinny man can be a visual picture of how people sometimes trade in things of eternal beauty and consequence for a few pennies. We can talk about the spiritual poverty that tempts us to do this.

Keep smiling. Consider yourself on a treasure hunt trying to uncover a grand story. It is such a wonderful experience to elicit a story or piece of their history that you've never heard before. How wonderful to share the wealth of your find with families. Being careful to maintain the boundaries of confidentiality, it can be wonderfully heart-warming for families to hear stories that the person you visited shared with you. However small those memories may be, they remind the families that their loved ones are still there! That person is their father, mother, brother, parent and they have not forgotten those memories. For them to hear them as stories remembered is wonderfully healing for them.

Think of conversations with dementia patients as being cumulative. Perhaps you do have the same conversation as your last visit. It is just as meaningful to that person this time as it was last time! What is even more important is that you are touching the lives of that family as well. Many of them show up day after day to face the same conversations over and over again, to provide what little comfort they can in the face of an illness that robs their loved one daily of memories and abilities.

Since the person suffering from dementia may not remember your visit, particularly in the advanced stages of dementia, leave some evidence of your visit for the family to discover; a copy of your most recent church newsletter, a business card with the date of your visit (if there is already one there, leave another one), a church bulletin, a note on the dry erase boards saying hello, a flower from the communion table, a little craft etc. Some families leave a guest book. Don't be shy about signing it and putting a little note of encouragement or saying something about the visit. Often families who have been dealing with a person who has dementia will gradually pull away from attending their faith communities regularly. Some are embarrassed by the behaviours of their loved ones, many find there are physical barriers and become exhausted by the level of care that is required. Since many will have to wait months or even years to get into a long-term care facility, often the opportunity to attend church can be disrupted. It means much when someone calls to say they visited a loved one.

They are naked!

It's OK. You are not going to see anything that God didn't create. Remember that if they realized that they were naked, they wouldn't be naked. You are witnessing what it must have been like in the garden of Eden before Adam and Eve realized their nakedness and the shame that often seems to be present.

First of all, do your best to avoid the problem by not going behind closed curtains without calling over the curtain first to see if the patient or resident is receiving personal care. If they are, ask when you should return. Before entering the room, knock and enter in tentatively so that if the patient is undressed and didn't hear you, you can back out until they are ready to receive you. Many residents and patients forget to close the doors when they are in the washroom so be aware of this as you enter. Often your nose will tell you if this is the case. Use your instincts.

If you can see before you enter into the room that the resident is naked, you can ask the nurse or support staff member to cover them so they are ready to receive you. If they are sleeping and there is sheet or blanket easily available, you can cover them and then wake them gently for the visit.

If they begin to strip during the course of your visit, calmly intervene by telling them quietly not to remove their clothing. If you see them begin to undress, gently hold their hands and distract them with conversation. This takes away their hands from unbuttoning their clothes and pulling their arms through their sleeves. It may allow you to continue your visit. Reaching out to shake their hand and continuing to shake their hand during the course of the conversation often works as well. Sometimes they remove clothing for a reason they are having trouble vocalizing. They may be removing clothing because they are hot and can't connect the feeling with words. Try asking them if they are feeling hot. If they indicate that they are, you could help them remove outer sweaters and top blankets to see if that stops the behaviour. If there is a fan in the room or the ability to open the window, you could try this as well. Keep in mind that the buildings are temperature controlled so be sure to close the window prior to leaving. If the patient or resident is able to drink, you could also offer them a cool drink. They may need to use the washroom. Ask and if the answer is yes, assist them to find a staff member.

Remember, you've decided that you aren't going to be disturbed by someone who is naked but sometimes families cannot overcome their embarrassment. There are a couple of options. Without anxiety or panic, just simply offer to come back and visit at another time. Before you leave, shake the hand of the person who is naked and thank them for the visit. This is what you would do if they were clothed. Do not take away their dignity by failing to attempt this gesture, then turn to other family members and thank them as well. If the visit doesn't seem completed, I offer to move the visit to another place; a family room, staff lounge, coffee shop or even the hallway if they are concerned about keeping an eye on their loved one. Do not stop visiting them because of this or any other behaviour or you will only reinforce the family's sense of embarrassment or shame.

They Can't Follow Directions

Many residents may not be able to handle multiple directions, answer multiple questions or handle questions that are complex. For instance, if you take someone for coffee and ask what they would like to drink, they may not remember what the options are. You may want to instead ask them if they would like a cold drink or a hot drink. Once they have answered that question, then offer them coffee or tea. Instead of asking them what they take in their coffee, you might want to ask if they would like sugar in their coffee and then wait for the answer. Also ask if they would like milk and then wait for the answer. It takes a few minutes longer, but preserves the dignity of choice. For those whose language skills are really impaired, you can ask them to point to what they would like to have.

If you want to try a little experiment, try asking each person you meet (who you assume doesn't speak), "How are you today (insert name)?" Wait for 30 seconds and say it again. Wait for a minute and say it a third time. I think you will be shocked by the number of people who will verbally answer if you give them enough time.

In the same way, if you are guiding someone while walking, instead of saying, "Let's make a right turn when we get off the elevator to go to the car," break it down into, "Step off the elevator;" after they have stepped off the elevator, say, "Turn right;" once they have turned right, direct them towards the car. Remember that many seniors have low vision, so be aware of anything that they might trip over, such as curbs or even a little water on the floor.

It's Boring to Visit Them

I'm not surprised you are bored. I suspect if they were able to communicate better they would tell you that you are boring them by reading the same passages every visit. Why not read some of the wonderful stories, the exciting trip across the desert, the amazing miracles, the incredible saga of Paul, the wonderful words of *the rest of* the Psalms (not just the 23rd). In any ministry, if you are bored, so are the people who you are caring for. If you are bored with your sermon, the likelihood that those listening to it are finding it exciting is probably small. It is the same with visiting. Regardless of the person or the illness, you must find a meaningful way to connect. What were their interests growing up? Sports, music, animals, gardening, crafts, cars? What were the formative moments in their lives? Make a point of visiting them when their families are around so you can watch them communicate. Most families know what subjects are still viable for those suffering from dementia. Follow their lead.

Chapter 3

Palliative and Dying for Spiritual Care

Visiting patients who are palliative and dying are visits that scare many people the most. We are afraid we will say the wrong thing. Such patients force us to face our own death and we really aren't sure what to expect. One of the beautiful things about these visits, though, is that people are very real, and the conversations will be some of the most meaningful you will ever have.

It is important to not allow people to die a spiritual, emotional or social death before their physical death. Dying people are still living! They still have hopes and dreams, a "to-do" list, loved ones surrounding them. The normal ups and downs of life are still happening to them as they are dying. In short, their life isn't just about planning for their death, but also about dealing with difficult teenage children, finding daycare, paying the bills, getting their errands done, having their hearts broken and trying to live their lives. In the earliest part of the illness, it is important to assess all of these things in the same way we would for any home visit. Obviously, the illness that is threatening to shorten their lives will have an effect on all of these things, but don't give it any more or less energy than it deserves.

For instance, many chemo patients will suffer for extended periods of time with other undiagnosed illnesses simply because they have attributed their symptoms to the ongoing treatments rather than suspecting their symptoms might be something else. In the same way, we can attribute their spiritual distress, depression, anger as well as other emotions all coming from their attempts to cope with their diagnosis rather than seeing beyond to other issues in their lives.

In the last half century, the definition of palliative and dying have taken on significantly different meanings. Palliative and dying used to be defined in relatively short times, weeks to months. Now we are faced with people who may survive and thrive for decades, necessitating many decisions along the way and many conversations.

Imminently Dying

Clergy are often called upon when the person is imminently dying and only given hours or days to live. This is a very tender time in the life of a family. It is important to remember that people die as they live. If they were a miserly curmudgeon, chances are they will die that way. Many families have Hollywood movies in their mind showing great conversions, opportunities for closure and completely transformed relationships. Realistically, the changes rarely takes place in the dying patient but in the acceptance of family members as receiving the gift of learning that comes with every person who enters our life. Acknowledge those gifts with honesty, sensitivity and understanding. Should you have opportunity to do a funeral, bring that learning to that person's funeral. I think back to my own mother who suffered from high levels of anxiety throughout her life, often refusing to go to events or feeling so anxious that it was difficult for the rest of the family to enjoy when we did go. The gift in that was that she taught me how to be around extremely anxious people while remaining calm and reassuring. What a great gift to people who I meet under extreme trauma in emergency rooms, ICU's and in dying patients. We are the people who can help look for these gifts.

If you are called to attend to the family of someone who is imminently dying or has died, there are several tasks that are important. First, it is important to help the family remember who that loved one was in a way that is honest. If you don't have any background or you've never met the family before, then you can simply ask them to tell you about the person. Not all families will participate or be open to this but most are. Give them space to tell the stories. Ask questions that will continue to draw out their story as much as time and circumstances will allow. If you do know the person, then initiate the discussion by offering a memory from your own experience with this person. I really encourage telling a humourous story or one that draws out something that is significant for that person. Why? Because when we give them permission to laugh, we also give them permission to cry. Normally, in our culture, tears are not as socially acceptable as laughter except in the face of death where tears are the expectation. When we give them permission to laugh, we allow the grief to be expressed. The exception to this would be the death of an infant or very young child.

Once you have gathered the thoughts it is important to offer the family whatever rituals that are appropriate, whether prayers, anointing, readings from sacred literature, ceremonies etc. If your tradition lends itself to extemporaneous prayer and you feel comfortable doing this, then gather all of the thoughts that were shared by that family into your words and offer them back to God just as you offer the life of the person back to God.

Secondly, it is important to offer the patient and family the opportunity to talk about arrangements following death. Ideally, within the relationship the opportunity to discuss these arrangements has taken place much earlier in the continuum of care, but if it hasn't it can be raised. This may be a good time to talk about it, however, some families feel uncomfortable discussing arrangements in the presence of their loved ones. You can offer to move to another area but they may not want to move away from someone who is imminently dying. Discussing arrangements makes families feel that they are somehow hastening the death or putting a curse on their loved ones. I often acknowledge this vague feeling within their spirit by saying something like, "Sometimes families feel that they are hastening the death by talking about funeral arrangements." Just to have this acknowledged often makes the families look relieved. Reassure them that it is OK to talk about funeral arrangements.

Finally, ask the family if they have any questions? Many families don't know what the process is. It is best to keep things simply by telling families at this stage that the first decision that they will be asked to make is to name the funeral home that will be handling their arrangements. If they don't know, let them know that this is not a problem as they can go home and take all the time they need to think about it and advise the hospital or nursing home of their decision after they have had some time to think about it. The facility will keep the remains safe until that time. Reassure the family that if they make that one decision that the funeral directors and their clergy will walk them through all of the other decisions.

If you have more time prior to the death, helping families to think of those choices is a great service. What funeral home? Do they want burial or cremation? Who do they want to do the service? What hymns, reading, prayers, songs etc are meaningful for them? It is helpful to keep notes of stories and memories that they have shared with you if you are going to prepare a funeral.

Things to Never Say

One of the things that I never do in the workshops I lead is give a list of things to either say or not say during the course of visitation. The reason is quite simple; people and situations are incredibly complex. The reality is that if you choose to be involved in people's lives there will be times when you will make mistakes. You are only human. Even when we have said something that has caused an unpleasant reaction, there is still an opportunity to understand and explore that person's feelings.

One of the things that we should avoid is giving medical advice. Even if you have suffered the exact same diagnosis, refrain from giving advice. The reason for this is that it is important that we empower people to ask the questions that are on their mind to the doctors and others involved in their care. Secondly, it is important that we listen to patients to hear what THEIR understanding of their illness, treatment and prognosis are. This is often far more important. If you walk into emergency and the person has cut their hand in the kitchen and you say "a few stitches and you'll be good as new" and then walk out perhaps you've missed something. Was the cut the result of domestic abuse? Is the person terrified of needles, hospital or doctors? The level of physical trauma does not necessarily correlate to the level of spiritual or psychological trauma.

It is easy to assume we know how people feel. I mistakenly assumed that the loss of a pregnancy was a very sad event until one young woman had the courage to tell me how grateful she was not to be having a child at this time of her life.

Sometimes families reach the point in the illness where active treatment is no longer feasible. This is a particularly difficult stage for families, whether they have battled for a long time and are struggling to give up the fight or it has been a short time since an accident. It is difficult to absorb the reality that there is nothing more that can be done except keep the person comfortable. Families may have many feelings and anxieties around this time.

"I feel like we are starving them."

We spend a lifetime making sure that people eat, so it can be hard to reverse our thinking. Reassure the family that the body is shutting down and doesn't need or even want food. Ask them to think of a time when they had been sick and really, truly didn't want food or even the smell of the food. They were genuinely not hungry. As the body is dying it produces a natural endorphin that suppresses the feelings of hunger and pain. Similarly, palliative medications also prevent any feelings of discomfort associated with not eating. If the patient is awake and able to swallow, sometimes there is pleasure or comfort in putting a drop or two of a favourite soft food such as ice cream onto their tongue.

"Can they hear us?"

Absolutely. Now is a great time to talk to them about anything that is important to you. For some families this means that they wish to have discussions around withdrawal of treatment, funerals or any other discussion that they feel would be upsetting out of earshot. Some professionals would endorse this, feeling that it is unfair to patients to talk about them when they can't participate. Others feel that it is important to have those conversations with the person present. Either way, be attentive to the family's feelings.

"Are they in pain?"

First rule is to ask the patient. They may still be able to nod or moan in response to the question. If there is no verbal response, then the following signs might be an indication of pain: facial grimacing, rigidity, grabbing their blankets and clothing and various parts of their body, extreme restlessness, moaning or calling out that is not settled by comforting touch or redirected with conversation or music. It is normal for patients momentarily to exhibit these things especially when they are repositioned. However, if patients are continuously distressed, then call the medical staff to evaluate and let them know your observations. If you aren't seeing these things, then list the signs of pain out loud for the family and reassure them that they look comfortable and peaceful. If they do appear to be in pain, then empower the family to speak with their caregivers to correct the situation.

Withdrawal of Care – "I feel like I'm killing him."

As the time of death approaches, many families are faced with the decision as to whether or not they will continue with treatment. Within our health care system there can be so many options for care, that it can be overwhelming for families when the time comes that treatment is no longer indicated. Depending on the facility they may use one or more terms to delineate the direction that they are going.

DNR – Do not resuscitate. This generally means that when the heart stops, there will be no attempt to start it again. While this is clear, there can be many treatments that are to be considered before the heart finally stops.

AND – Allow natural death. This generally means that no active treatment will be offered and only comfort care will be given. It does not mean that the patient will not receive any medication. Many families are worried that a natural death means that no analgesics (pain medication) will be offered. Any medication or treatment that promotes comfort and quality of life will be considered or continued.

Comfort/Palliative Measures. This generally means that we will no longer provide treatment that will prolong life but will offer treatments that allow patients to die comfortably.

Euthanasia. This is not legally allowed in Canada. The assurance that you can offer families is that staff will not be offering a treatment that would hasten the death of the patient, or prescribing medication that would not be in the patient's best interests.

Regardless of the decisions, often we are asked as caregivers whether or not the family is making a decision that is ethical and allowed within their theological understanding. You need to be prepared to answer these questions. Your reaction to these questions will weigh heavily.

In my experience, there is guilt on either side of any decision. If the family continues treatment, they may feel guilty that they have kept the person alive and suffering. If they choose to withdraw treatment, they may feel guilty thinking that they killed their loved ones and didn't give them another chance. Sharing this information with the family this can be helpful by normalizing these feelings.

Withdrawal of Life Support (WLS). This means that anything that is used to artificially keep the person alive is discontinued either partially or completely. This may include a respirator (breathing machine), dialysis, medication to sustain blood pressure and heart rate among others, oxygen, feeding tubes or IV therapy. Sometimes families choose to withdraw everything at once and other times they choose to do it in stages.

Some people will be resistant to withdrawal, hoping for a miracle and the challenge is to balance a realistic prognosis with the expression of faith. Sometimes we are tempted to play it safe and just pray for the miracle and healing rather than assist the family to accept the reality of the situation. As you support families in these difficult situations, be aware of your own values and emotions so that you are able to bring clarity and wisdom to this difficult time of making decisions.

Chapter 4
Mental Health Issues

First of all, if you know people in your congregation who are hospitalized or suffer from mental health issues then you are in a very privileged place because many of the patients that I meet don't want anyone to know about their illnesses. They are afraid of the stigma that comes with mental illness and are doubly afraid that their faith community will further label their illness as a sign of a lack of faith or a failure on their part to pray, live or follow God's will correctly.

The first place that we need to visit people suffering from mental illness is from the pulpit. How often do we pray for broken limbs and bodies but forget to pray for broken minds and spirits? Be specific in your list of prayers by praying for all those who suffer from depression, thoughts of suicide, anxiety, reoccurring thoughts and nightmares, obsessive-compulsive behaviour, anorexia and addictions, just to name a few. Be careful in your sermons not to label mental health issues as failures. Encourage a spirit of openness and honesty and do not put people on display if they choose to share.

Secondly, we need to keep doing what we are doing and do it better. Studies have shown that those who are part of a faith community are less likely to suffer from mental illness and those who have a faith community are less likely to suffer a relapse and require less hospitalizations throughout the course of their lives. While there are different theories as to why, there are several things that faith communities are good at that promote optimal mental health. First, we encourage regular participation in the life of the community and have varying levels of engagement to meet the different needs. You can sit at the back of a Sunday service and slip out without anyone noticing you or you can participate in every group. Secondly, we tend to offer food at many of our gatherings which promote mental health and encourages socialization. The predictable routine of a church can offer structure to those who are suffering from mental health issues. Having said all that, part of our visitation should be to optimize and encourage the participation of those who may be on the edges due to mental health. It is a fine balancing act between being the person who encourages participating to tolerance and the person who walks with them until they can launch successfully back into their lives.

Depression

Depression is the "common cold" of mental health challenges. Spiritually speaking, one of the worst effects that depression can have on the person is they often feel like God has abandoned them, is punishing them or simply has lost interest in them. That is their lived experience and it is important for us not to challenge that so quickly that they feel ashamed for expressing this in the first place. Instead, create time and a place that allows the expression of honest feelings.

Secondly, in many cases depressions robs them of the ability to carry on normally. They may not have the energy to go to work, to participate in activities that they previously loved or to care for their families. Herein lies the challenge in spiritual care both to affirm them their feelings and the normalcy of their experience and at the same time gently encourage them to begin to participate and slowly reintegrate back into the community. In the same way that we would provide support to those suffering from a broken bone we must do the same for those suffering from depression.

Hallucinations, Visions and Thought Disturbances

For people struggling with acute mental health issues, hallucinations, visions and thought disturbances are part of the symptoms. The intensity of these symptoms can be very frightening, both for the person experiencing them and for the person who is observing. Once again, spiritual care says that we need to attend to those who are suffering from mental health issues.

When speaking with people who are in the acute phase of their illness sometimes their images are material that we can work with and need to be attended to. One young man who I spoke with talked about angels around him. The medical staff had dismissed and discouraged him from talking about his experiences with angels. In the initial part of the interview, the man was extremely agitated and animated but as he began to share how the angels had stopped him from jumping over the balcony or told him to stop taking a dangerous combination of drugs and alcohol, it became clear that these visions had a meaningful purpose in his life. As I began to acknowledge that purpose, he calmed down to the point where the conversation lost all of the dysfunctional behaviour that was displayed at the beginning. Similarly, a man described his search for the holy grail. When we began to talk about this image as a metaphor for his search for meaning and belonging in a world that rejected him, the conversation changed dramatically.

Having said that, it is important in all aspects of visitation to ensure your safety with people who may have strange behaviours and could cause you injury. Be aware of your surroundings and aware of people who may strike out in their dementia or hallucinations.

The gift of listening is a powerful gift in the lives of those we visit and even more so for those who suffer from mental health issues. Some additional time may be life-changing for those who are struggling with mental health issues.

Chapter 5

Hospital Visits

Hospital visits are some of the most important visits that will happen in your ministry. It can take you months or even years to get to know a family in your community but put them in hospital for a few days and visit them and you will come to know them and establish a bond with them that will be unique and strong. Seeing families through a lifetime of weddings and funerals, sickness and health, job loss and successes is one of the graces of ministry. Nowhere is the foundation laid more strongly than in a person who comes to visit someone who is in hospital. Make hospital visitation a priority in your ministry. Not only does it help to forge relationship but it challenges your theology. If your theology can stand up in the emergency room, it will probably hold together better in the pulpit.

Infection Protection

Almost daily there is an article in the newspaper that highlights the importance of infections. Nosocomial (health-care acquired) infections are an increasing and difficult problem that cannot be ignored. We want to ensure that our visits do not put those in our care at increased risk for acquiring secondary infections. In addition, we also want to ensure the protection of those who are doing this very important work, so that their health is not jeopardized.

The absolute most important thing in health care and visiting today is to wash your hands. Never mind all that foot washing! Hand washing is the most important thing that you can do. You should wash your hands as you come into hospital, before you enter the room, if you come in contact with any bodily fluids during your visit (putting a wafer on the tongue of the patient counts), and after you leave the room. If you are in a semi-private or ward room, and you want to offer care to the person in the next bed, you should wash your hands before moving to the next bedside. Just because you haven't touched the patient does not mean that you have not come in contact with their environment.

Look for signage that indicates that the patient may be in "Contact Precautions" which means that you should be wearing Personal Protective Equipment (PPE). This could include gown, gloves, mask (surgical or N95) or some form of eye protection. The order with which you put the items on does not matter but the order that you remove them is.

Before you touch any of the PPE, wash your hands.

Put on your gown on. It should be tied at the back so that if you sit down, you don't pick up bugs on your clothes.

Surgical masks are placed over the ears with the metal part at the top molded around the bridge of the nose. For N95 masks, place the mask on your face with the metal portion to the top. Pull the elastic over the top of your head. It is often easier to remove your glasses while doing this. Press hard on this metal part to form fit the mask around your nose. All of the air that you are breathing should come through the mask. Those people who wear glasses have a natural test; if your glasses steam up while you are wearing it, it is not fitted properly. Some hospitals offer the opportunity for spiritual care providers to have their N95 masks professionally fitted. It is worthwhile to attend one of these sessions because once you understand how the mask works, you have a better sense if the mask is fitted properly. Since there are several different styles of masks, the mask fitting sessions will also identify if one style doesn't work for you and give you a card indicating which mask and size is best suited to you. These certificates are normally valid for two years and it is advisable that you carry it with you whenever you are visiting to ensure you wear the correct mask. Keep in mind that the mask may not fit properly if you have a weight gain or loss of 10 or more pounds or if you have facial hair or a facial injury.

When you remove the equipment, the order in which you take it off and the method is important. All protective equipment should be removed inside the room and disposed of inside the room. In some hospitals that are cramped for space, sometimes the disposal units are just outside the doors. On the very rare occasion a patient may be in double isolation, where there is a room in-between the patient's room and the hallway that has negative pressure for removing PPE prior to exiting.

The basic idea is that you do not carry any contaminants outside of the room. Remove the gloves first turning them inside out as you remove them and trying to touch the outside as little as possible. Dispose of them in the garbage. Next remove the gown again turning it inside out and rolling it to minimize touching the outside. If it is a disposable gown, put it in the garbage. If it is one that is laundered, put it in the laundry bin inside the room. Wash your hands. If you are wearing goggles, remove them first and dispose of them in the appropriate container. Wash your hands (yes again). Hold the mask with one hand, pull the elastic over the top of your head until the elastics are in front of you. Remove mask and dispose in garbage. Wash your hands one more time and then exit the room. Be sure to finish your conversation before you begin this process because you cannot step back into the room for a last goodbye or threshold conversation. If you need to leave the room for any reason, you must remove all of the PPE and don it again before you come back in no matter how many times.

One dying patient in full contact precautions had a large family around his bedside. I offered them some water and two people said they would like some so I took off the PPE and obtained the water and re-gowned and gloved and went back in with the water. Once I returned a few more people thought that was a good idea and so it went. Yes, it was frustrating but contaminating the ice and water machine could have had grave consequences. If you need something such as water, tissues or assistance from staff, you can ring the call bell and ask them to bring them or stand at the threshold of the doorway and flag someone down but do not leave the room while still in your PPE.

Don't visit people if you are sick or think you might be sick. A benign cold to a healthy person can be a devastating pathogen to someone who is already ill, older or immune-compromised. If three or more residents in any facility are suddenly ill, samples are sent to labs and the Public Health can shut down the entire facility to all visitors and cancel all plans for residents to leave the building. All parties that would bring residents together are cancelled, all activities that involve sharing of items or making food are cancelled and residents who are sick are confined to their rooms for many days and residents who share the same home area where there is an outbreak, must remain in that home area until the outbreak is declared over by Public Health. In addition, they cannot move between floors or units nor can volunteers or families visit.

Since staff must take care of residents, many of them will become ill too. Each time there is a new case, the Public Health extends the deadline for the outbreak, meaning that the situation can go on for weeks or months. Since many residents don't have the cognitive capacity to remember to stay in their room, cover their mouths or toilet themselves an outbreak is difficult to contain. Just as the helping hands of volunteers and family are barred from the facility, the care needs of residents are skyrocketing on a team of people that is also a risk for succumbing to the same illness. Since residents and patients are so medically vulnerable and have so many health problems, the death rate during outbreaks is often higher. During one particularly bad outbreak in a home, every resident lost either a spouse, roommate or tablemate. The grief in the building was overwhelming. I hope that if you didn't appreciate the importance of not visiting while you are sick at the beginning of this chapter that you do now. This is so important, I'm going to reiterate it. Please, do not visit if you are sick.

If you must visit someone who is sick or in isolation, be aware of anything that you bring into the rooms. If the room is in isolation, you should try to avoid bringing anything in. Leave your valuables in your car. In most places you could leave other things at the nursing station for safekeeping during your visit. Anything that you do take into the room should remain tucked under your gown. If it is something that you need to use during the course of your visit, then it should be wiped down with a disinfectant cloth before you leave the room or as soon as possible after. Often the containers of disinfectant cloths look like the same containers that contain baby wipes. Since the disinfectants can be strong, you may wish to put another glove on to handle them (don't forget to wash your hands before you reach in the glove box again...I know it feels like insanity but remember that patients lives depend on this!)

If possible bring religious paraphanalia that is disposable (i.e. communion cups) and if you are bringing holy oils or waters, remember not to "double dip". This means that you wash your hands immediately before you touch your holy oil and you don't dip your hand or your fingers back into the oil after you have touched the patient or their environment, otherwise you are now carrying around a vial of infectious material.

How Long Should I Visit?

This is one of the questions that I am most frequently asked and the traditional advice has been 20 minutes. However I disagree. For someone who is very ill, that time frame might be 18 minutes too long, while someone who is in psychiatry may need a couple of hours of your time to unpack the complex issues and feelings and family issues that are relevant to their situation. When I evaluate the statistics of my students, I express concern if I don't see a variety of different lengths of time that they spent with patients. If they only log a few minutes for each patient they see, then I challenge them to evaluate whether or not they are addressing the issues and how can they make their visits deeper.

Sometimes it takes great courage to have a meaningful conversation, to move the conversation between the weather and the deep personal challenges that life brings and so I challenge my students to do this. I also express concern if they only have long visits wondering if they may be missing cues that indicate that the patient is ready to terminate the visit sooner. In general, patients who are in the Emergency department (ED), the Intensive Care Unit (ICU), Critical Care Unit (CCU) or are undergoing treatment that makes them nauseated or tired such as chemotherapy tend to prefer shorter visits or prefer you to visit them in your prayers or with a card. With parking lots filled to capacity at most hospitals, it can be frustrating to fight the weather, traffic and parking and not feel that you want to have at least a 20 minute visit. Do not make your visit a function of the length of time it takes to get parking. This goes for home visiting as well. Do not assume that because you are in a home the person is feeling any more up to visiting than in other settings.

How Do I Know When It is Time to Leave?

There can be many clues. Sometimes people will try to conclude a visit by thanking you for coming.

They may continually glance at the door. They may shift in their beds or pull their blankets up higher. If they are nodding off or appearing tired or worn or there may be more lulls in the conversation. If in doubt, ask! It's the simplest solution. If you are planning on visiting on another day, this is one of the best ways to phrase the question, "Mrs. Smith, you seem tired, would you like me to stay or would you like me to come back another day?" Keep in mind that some people are shy about kicking out someone from their faith community, especially clergy (that's like kicking God out isn't it?) so you still need to be attuned to the body language, but it is important to enlist the person's feedback. Remember if you are promising to visit another time, it is really important to follow through on that promise. Even residents with severe memory issues will often remember that you promised to visit.

Also, consider people who are lonely or institutionalized often hear "mights" as "will" and "maybes" as "definitely." In other words, you say that "you might visit next Tuesday" and the lonely person in hospital hears that as "you will visit next Tuesday." You communicate that "maybe" the ladies will come by next week with cookies and the resident plans an entire tea party because you will "definitely" be there next week.

When to Visit

For hospitals, whenever possible, it is always advisable to follow the posted visitation rules. Most hospitals have visitation on most wards in the afternoon and early evening. Outside of these hours, patients are often being given personal care making visitation awkward. If it is a crisis situation, hospitals welcome the support that you can offer to families outside of these hours but please be prepared to be patient with staff who will have tests and tasks to accomplish during your visit.

Chapter 6

Residential Facilities

For long-term care and other home-like institutions, the emphasis is on cultivating normalcy, so we encourage you to visit the way you would have prior to the resident coming into long-term care, taking into account the limitations of the resident. Did you normally spend the afternoon playing cards or drinking tea and boring them with photographs of your latest vacation? Feel free to play cards or bring five thousand photographs. The goal in long-term care is to normalize their lives as much as possible, and visitors are an important part of that philosophy.

I believe that long-term care facilities are a great place to train children for visitation. Our youngest official volunteer started when she was five and now brings her three younger brothers and sisters along. The residents love them! When the residents have the opportunity to go to their home church and you see these small children running up to greet them with such joy and excitement; it is something special. They aren't afraid of wheelchairs or people who are older and have behaviours that they might not have encountered otherwise. These early experiences for children are a good foundation for experiences later in life that otherwise might overwhelm them.

It is great that our medical care has pushed life expectancy into the eighties but it also means that young people are much older when someone they love dies. They are often missing those early childhood experiences of death to help teach them how to cope and what to do. Visitation in nursing homes is one way of teaching children many life skills about aging, living, death and dying. The stories that residents can tell about the War Years, surviving the depression, raising young children without a partner, gardening to survive are wonderful ways to relate to young children. You may also be able to bring pets with you for visits. There are some residents I wouldn't visit unless I had the dog with me!

If you have a calm animal that has had all of its shots, and a personality that is amenable to visits, it can be a great ice-breaker and a wonderful way of visiting. Prior to bringing the animal, check with staff to see if pets are allowed. You do not have to have a calm, well behaved child however as the residents find children who are misbehaving much more interesting to watch and talk about later! They will also have lots of parenting advice and often some great words of encouragement. Finally, don't forget to ask the resident what they would like to do. Some of the options are going for a walk (be sure to check with staff and sign the resident out), coffee (be sure that there are no swallowing or dietary issues), communion, reading or a favourite activity. One church's ministry was simply to bring a box of cards, stamps, pen and paper and assist the resident to write notes or Christmas cards to family and friends. Many residents miss their friends in the community or living in other institutions. Any attempts to bring them together or connect them brings tears of joy.

For visitation at home, it is often challenging as so many people are discharged from hospital with significant recovery still ahead that spiritual caregivers need to be very sensitive to their particular situation if you are visiting someone who is ill. Home visitation is more effective if is something that is all encompassing, not just something that happens during crisis. The more that we normalize visiting at home, the less awkward it will feel when crises are happening.

Consider visiting in groups. If your faith community would like to do something special for patients or residents, it is always best to check with the spiritual or recreation department or the community coordinator to see if your plans are appropriate within the setting. Consider importing one of the churches favourite activities to a local residential setting. Some examples are: sewing, quilting, singing, musical or drama productions, choirs, games nights, movies, pot-luck meals, church services, crafts, computers and other interests. On one occasion, the men's groups who build model trains set up their train display at the facility. At first they couldn't get it going but there were residents there to help! How great it was to see them participating and problem solving and celebrating when it got started! Then the residents streamed down to see the display. In order to be successful, coordinate with the facility well in advance so that they have staff available to assist and are set-up for you.

Use caution before purchasing any items for donation. One church purchased a number of large candy canes to be delivered to each patient in the hospital, dropping them off in my office. They were very hurt and offended that as a department of one I didn't have the time to deliver them. They didn't understand that in order to do this, I would have to check the charts of every patient prior to delivery to ensure that they didn't have any swallowing difficulties, a medical condition such as diabetes or weren't NPO (nothing by mouth) for upcoming tests or surgery. Two units were under quarantine, making the delivery a risk to both staff and patients of spreading something other than Christmas cheer. They were absolutely well meaning but if they had checked with me, I had two children in hospital from the same family following a fire who didn't have warm clothes to leave the hospital with or toys for Christmas. I spent the week "borrowing" from the funds of local churches to give this family the basics. I could have applied the money used to buy candy canes to help a family in a very meaningful way. Other groups have purchased equipment to donate, only to find out that we can't accept it due to health care regulations and safety rules that they had not taken into consideration.

When this is coordinated correctly, churches have done really meaningful work. Patients love the band that plays once a month at hospital. On one occasion, a local church made fifty blankets and hosted a Christmas party for the long-term patients in the hospital. They didn't put any gift tags on them and allowed them to choose their colour and style. What a wonderful simple dignity – the dignity of choice. One woman was so delighted because she had a new grandchild. She had been confined to hospital for over two years and didn't have the funds to purchase a gift for that child. As with any grandparent, she wanted to give a gift to the child. It was the greatest desire of her heart. She chose a blanket not for herself but for her grandchild.

How Can We Help Them Transition?

Going to a residential care facility is a very difficult decision for both the resident and their families. Many families wish to continue to care for their loved ones in their own home but it is just not possible, and relinquishing care to another facility or person sometimes feel like a defeat. Many families feel overwhelmed with guilt over the decision and often their guilt doesn't dissipate with time, even though the resident has adjusted well to the facility. There are some things that churches can do to help ease the transition.

First of all – visit. Many churches don't visit in the early stages of admission because the resident can be quite upset and tearful. Of course they are tearful! They have reduced their entire home to just a few boxes and a few hundred square feet. They've lost much of their independence, enough of their health to require 24 hour nursing care and probably got a phone call yesterday telling them if they wanted to have the room, they had to move today, quite possibly having waited months if not years for the space.

Researching this early time of admission, the tears represented two other things; first of all that they would be cut off from their friends and communities and secondly they were sad to see their friends and family leave after visiting, their tears a sign of anticipatory grief. Visiting early in the process provides much needed reassurance that they have not lost those important connections and you do accept their feelings of anger, sorrow, loss, frustration and confusion. In the lives of families, the day of admission and the week following is one of the most difficult, particularly for families who have residents who don't see their need for long-term care and may not be able to remember that they were coming to long-term care. Can you imagine how you would feel if someone picked you up to take you to lunch and you never went home again? Can you imagine how difficult it is to watch your own family member cry and beg to be taken home?

What Should We Talk About?

It seems strange to me that we take great delight in telling the same stories over and over again to children and yet find it boring to repeat the same conversation or stories with our seniors. And yet, if we are open to it, we can take just as much delight in hearing seniors' stories and encourage them to vocalize the same sentences and phrases that bring them delight. Each morning, one resident tells me how beautiful I look today (no matter how many times I walk past him – how cool is that). Another calls me "shortie" while I remind him that since he's closer to God, I expect him to show up at my church service for the day. He laughs like he's never heard that one before (if only my parishioners would laugh at my sermon jokes that way)! Then there is the woman who is "always, always good." I will always miss the gentleman who was smoking in my parking spot every morning, the woman who had a "Presbyterian peppermint" in a blue Crown Royal bag (not that she drank she would cautiously remind me). Take delight in the repetition, the familiar, the nuggets of gold offered to you.

If you find it onerous to start conversations, bring along a conversation starter. Pictures are wonderful or a little newspaper article that you read. If you want to steer the conversation to something more spiritual, bring along a little something from your devotions or a prayer that you read. What are the resident's interests? One dear person who is now "accessorizing" in heaven couldn't be happier than when you took her shopping or asked her opinion about clothing, make-up or jewellery. "The most important accessory a woman can have is a man." Yes we did get around to some deep spiritual conversations but if our sole focus is religious conversation and jargon, we miss a lot of souls.

Many people's spirituality is expressed in their gardens, families, charity work, fishing and the golf course. If we took the time to really hear how God is speaking to them in the places they are, they will surprise us with their insights and knowledge.

Chapter 7

Responding to Trauma

Just as I was writing this chapter, a train derailment happened in Burlington, killing three and sending dozens of people to various area hospitals.

From time to time, we may be called on to visit families during extremely traumatic events. Things can happen very quickly and it can be difficult to keep your bearings, especially since these events are relatively rare in the lives of most people.

During the initial phase when families are first told the news of what has happened or is happening, they may react with extreme emotion including crying, throwing themselves on the floor, fainting, vomiting, throwing fists at walls, screaming etc. Since we don't often attend to these events, we may be tempted to try and stop or control these reactions. Allow the family the time to express these very deep and raw emotions. It can be extremely uncomfortable to be there but also important. Some people are tempted to step out of the room but that confers the message that their emotions are unacceptable and/or you are afraid of them (which you may very well be but spiritual care reminds us that we are called to be present). By all means if the family requests privacy, step out of the room and let them know you will wait for them close by. Don't panic, as one of my classmates used to say, "Calm, non-anxious presence, oh yea, that's suppose to be me."

Sometimes my students will wonder if the families are out of control. There is one simple test that can put your minds at ease. What happens when the cell phones ring or text messages are received? If you watch closely, most people will stop reacting long enough to answer them and deal with them.

This is not to say that the reaction is not real but that the person is still in control.

Secondly, in just about every family, there is a leader who will signal to the family when to grieve and how long to grieve. This is not done consciously on their part but you can use this person to help you work with the family. Watch the family dynamics closely and utilize that person's authority within the family to help the family move through their grief and accomplish the tasks that need to be done, especially those tasks that police, fire and medical personnel are requiring at that time. You can often identify this person because whenever they speak or signal, the crying and emotional reactions temporarily cease.

During this initial stage, the family's ability to hear and understand and process what is happening is severely limited. If you are in the room at the time, you can help the family keep track of information. Write down important information, the name of the doctor, police officer or other person who spoke with them. Write down any contact information or critical information such as the diagnosis and treatment plan, location of people and bodies as well as the names of people who may be able to answer their questions. They are probably not able to think of the important questions at this time but this will be important later.

As you have more experience in dealing with these situations, you learn what is important for families to know. If you can think of questions that would be important for the family, speak up and ask them. Be very careful not to ask the questions that you are curious about or questions that will unnecessarily further traumatize the family. For instance, many traumatic deaths are also Coroner's cases. This means that the coroner has control in the investigation and will determine if there is any access to the body and if an autopsy will be necessary amongst other things. Obviously this can have a huge impact on the family's grief and funeral arrangements so these are examples of a valid questions: "When do you anticipate releasing the body to the funeral home?" or "Will the family be able to view the body?" or "Is the body in a state that is appropriate for viewing?" Asking the police where the decapitated head landed on the highway is an example of a question that will probably further traumatize those in the room and is information that isn't needed at that time.

These situations often have media attention surrounding them and it can be helpful to let the family know that the media often doesn't get the events correctly and/or will sensationalize them. Sometimes families will not feel that they can refuse to answer questions and this is where you can reassure them that they do not need to speak to the media or answer questions that are intrusive. Some members of the family find meaning in speaking with the media if they feel that there is something to be learned from their situation that will prevent a similar tragedy. This is one way that families make sense out of senseless situations and it may bring them some meaning. If this is the case, it can be helpful to encourage the family to wait until they are a little more stabilized and help them to sort out what they want to say and which questions will be off limits.

Once the initial reaction has passed, you can begin to help the family prioritize. You may need to be directive at this stage as they often don't know what needs to happen first. Help them to think of who might need to be contacted or located. It is sometimes helpful to suggest that they hold off on contacting people outside of the immediate circle as this tends to mean that as they arrive, the initial reactions starts all over again. If the family is not in their own home then moving a large group of people from the hospital can be difficult. Assist them to find people who might answer any immediate questions that they might have. Think about arranging transportation and looking after their immediate needs. Are there any diabetics in the group who haven't eaten in a while? Are there any family members who might be especially sensitive to this situation due to an existing problem?

Clergy and the people from faith communities come to these situations with a greater understanding of the family situation that can be invaluable. Use your knowledge of that family and their dynamics to help them. Offer to go with them to their homes, hospital, police station, the morgue or any other place the situation might take them. Think critically of other people in the church who might be able to assist with picking up children from school, rides, care-giving responsibilities, meals and support. Who in the church is closest to them who would be least intrusive? Offer to call these people.

Often in these situations, families are asked to make horrendous decisions regarding withdrawal or not continuing with treatment. It is usually easier for families to elect to not continue treatment rather than to begin a treatment and then be faced with withdrawing some time later.

Regardless, there is guilt and anxiety and questioning on either side of any choice under these circumstances. Telling the family this, may help them to clear the emotional baggage to make a logical decision. It makes the families feel like they are killing their loved one rather than allowing them to die naturally. It can be helpful to the family to ask them what the patient would have wanted if they were able to voice their own wishes? If as a visitor, you have had a conversation with this person that would offer some insight, then it is appropriate to offer this. Many families at this stage, can't fathom the loss and are in a tremendous amount of shock. They may not be able to make a decision and sometimes this means that the medical team will hold off for a period of time from withdrawing care to allow the family some time to adjust or sometimes to wait until other family members arrive.

Families perceive you as "God's ambassador" so be very aware of your words. You do not want to offer families false hope, or words that make them feel as though they are being judged.

ORGAN DONATION

Organ donation is another difficult topic that comes up. There are two legal ways to die in Canada, either your heart or your brain stops. Most people understand that if your heart stops, you are dead.

Brain death is more difficult for families to understand. For a time period, after the brain stops, through the use of medical technology, we can continue to keep the other vital organs functioning, opening up the possibility of donation. Should we turn-off or withdraw that technology, the heart and other organs will stop, however, the person has already died because their brain has died. Sometimes the team will approach the family because the patient is already brain dead or they see that their injuries are such that they believe that the person is moving towards brain death. If all of the tests have been done and the person has been declared brain dead, then the family may be given the option of organ donation if the circumstances of the death do not preclude this (certain diseases, severe trauma to other organs).

In order to ascertain if the donor is a good candidate, the questions that are asked of the family are highly personal so you may wish to offer the family some privacy to answer them. If there are children in the room, then this might be the time to suggest a trip to the coffee shop. If the person is moving towards brain death, then the team may ask permission of the family to run certain tests in the event that the brain death does occur. These tests will not interfere or change the care that the patient is receiving but will help hospital staff to make the best use of the organ donation in the event that brain death becomes a reality.

Depending on the hospital and the area, some hospitals will do donation after cardiac death (DACD). What this means is that the patient's brain is severely injured but did not die. They will never make a recovery to sustain life and the person is dependent on machines and medication to live. Families may elect to withdraw care and allow the person to die naturally. The person will then most likely die a cardiac (heart) death. Should the person die within a set time frame, which differs between hospitals, then the person may still donate. If they don't die within the timeframe, they will be moved back to a room in the hospital for palliative care.

Sometimes families want privacy during this time and sometimes they find it meaningful to have clergy present, praying, reading or just being a silent witness to the transition from life to eternal life. Regardless of the circumstances, many families look to clergy to clarify religious beliefs and ethics around donation. To the best of my knowledge there are no religious groups that ban or discourage organ donation. A donation can save up to eight lives and potentially improve the quality of life for others. If it is the person's expressed wish that they did not want to donate, then it should be honoured. If it is the family's wish not to donate, then they should not feel pressured.

Helping families with viewings at the hospital can be another task of the spiritual caregiver. Arrange to meet the family at the hospital. If possible, try to seat them together in a quiet place until you are ready to proceed. Often there is a chapel or designated spiritual centre than can be used for this purpose. Arrange with staff to have the body brought to the viewing area. Many hospitals require certain people to be present depending on the circumstances so it may take time for those people to be notified.

BEFORE you take the family to the viewing area, it is important that you go yourself first. The first purpose for this is for you to get over the shock of seeing the body so that you can better assist the family. Make sure that it is the right body. When you see the body, make sure that it is as presentable as possible. If there are traumatic injuries that can be covered up with a sheet, then do so. Sometimes it is helpful to bring out the hand from underneath the sheet. If it is a coroner's case, then some tubes may have to be left in or you may not be allowed to touch the body at all. Make sure that there are tissues and chairs available and that you have a prayer or reading in case this is requested. When you return to the family, give them an idea of what they will see; bruises, tubes that remain in, wounds etc. Remind them, that they don't have to go if they wish to remain in the room. Ask the family if they would like to go together as a group or if they would like to split into smaller groups. Which family members would like to have a moment alone with the deceased? If this is the case, step outside of the room and remain in the general vicinity. Sometimes families have a tremendously difficult time leaving the body. Gentle words and prayers can ease the transition. Utilizing those leaders in the family to guide others who are struggling can be the key to helping families.

Finally, as you return to your places of worship be aware of the impact of vicarious trauma. Too often, pastors create additional work for themselves by traumatizing their congregations by either providing too many inappropriate details or not sharing enough information. Your first responsibility is to the family that you are helping. You must maintain confidentiality. If they give permission to share their story as part of a prayer request, consult with the family and think carefully about what you wish to share. You can say a "horrible car accident" instead of "horrible car accident that threw him through the windshield shearing his skin before landing on the road." In the same way, if you say, "the parishioner drowned in the lake" and that person was known for previous suicide attempts, you may unnecessarily cause the congregation to wonder if they missed some sign that this person was in trouble. However, had you said that "the parishioner died in the lake while fishing with his friends" the image is still difficult but different.

Expected vs Unexpected Deaths

It is important to remember expected deaths, even those of the very frail elderly or those who have suffered from a long standing illness will not necessarily evoke less emotions or grief than the traumatic deaths. I have watched families of young traumatic deaths react with remarkable calm and poise and clarity of thought and families of 99 year olds trigger a Code White because they reacted so violently to the news that their loved one had passed away and were certain that it was a failure of the medical staff. Don't assume even if you have a tremendous amount of history for the family that you will know what the trajectory of their grief will be. People that have "held it together" and you expect to continue on may suddenly collapse (physically or emotionally or spiritually) while those that seemed to struggle may suddenly rise up to meet the challenge. There are no stages to grief. Don't waste time trying to assess which stage they are at, just be prepared to respond to them as they are whether they are angry, depressed, accepting, hopeful, hopeless or all of these things at the same time and within moments of one another.

HELPING FAMILIES WITH MEDICAL DECISIONS

In traumatic circumstances, families are often called upon to make difficult decisions under confusing circumstances. Unfortunately most hospitals are set up to treat trauma patients, not to take care of the families who are awaiting news. The focus of the staff is on saving the person's life. Do nothing to add to the stress of the family. If you feel that the staff aren't being polite or professional, this is not the time to take up these things. By all means, at a later date or time but do not add to the burden of the family by putting another agenda on the table.

Ask for the hospital chaplain, social worker or volunteer to find out what they can about the patient.

Spiritual Care

They may be able to ask the team what information can they share with the family and provide a bit of an update which can help the family cope. They may be able to tell you which doctors are providing care and give you an estimate of when they will be able to come to speak with you. You can also ask if there is a private room for the family to gather in. Keep in mind that if the room is out of the way, they may prefer to stay in the immediate vicinity.

Often the medical team offers conflicting pictures or uses confusing jargon with family. If this is the case, you can ask for clarification or encourage the family to ask questions before the staff leave. If after leaving the room, the family begins to voice questions or concerns, you can request the staff member to return (once they are free) to answer some follow-up questions.

Once the patient has been stabilized the family may be allowed a short visit with the patient. You may accompany the family into the room. Patients who are critical may be transferred to other facilities for specialized care. Offering the family a ride is a great way to provide support. The patient may be transferred to a specialized unit such as Intensive Care, Pre-Op, Heart Investigation Units etc. All of these units have very strict visiting guidelines which they will relax if the patient is expected to die. If they aren't relaxing the rules, it means that the patient has a chance. Since there are many lines going into patients to infuse medication, hydrate, monitor and measure, the opportunity for infection is great, hence the need to minimize traffic and contact. Some units are limited to immediate family only.

While restrictions on visitation are extremely difficult on families, it also means that they can be encouraged to practice self-care. Since patients have a high level of care, reminding them that their loved one is well taken care of and staff will call if there is any changes may encourage them to go home. It is important for them to have rest and nutrition. Family who want to keep a vigil can be encouraged to do so in shifts, encouraging those in the crowd who have pre-existing medical conditions such as diabetes, recent surgeries, chemotherapy to go home first. Remind the family that recovery is a long process and the patient may need more help as they progress towards recovery.

WHEN TO LEAVE

One of the most difficult decisions that we have to make as caregivers is when to leave and when to come back in these situations. We don't want to leave prematurely and leave the families floundering and we don't want to stay and impose on their privacy and interfere with their abilities to utilize their own coping skills. There is no magic answer. Whatever you do, do not just come and do a prayer or a sacrament and leave unless the family is insistent that you go. I did show up at the hospital and the one family member ushered me to the bedside, insisted I pray quickly before her brother returned and saw that I was praying. Why? "Because he's one of those Bible thumping, Jesus freaks who will never shut up if he thinks I want a prayer for my mother!"

Leaving is not abandoning the family. In fact, it can send some very positive messages to the family.

It says that they are coping well enough that you can leave them for a time. It models the need for self-care. Spiritual caregivers and clergy do need to eat and sleep too! I read somewhere that one hour of spiritual care at the beginning of a crisis saves eight hours of counselling and care down the road. Trust that you have already given them so much in your presence. Finally, leaving ultimately says that we trust in God, however dim the way may seem right now. Over the coming days, and throughout the course of the illness, your presence has the potential to be transformative to those whom we serve.

Chapter 8
Dealing with Disabilities

The ability to deal with disabilities takes a little bit of persistence. Patience comes easily enough if we are willing to reflect for a moment on how lonely and difficult life must be if we suffer from a disability. Do your best to put yourself in the place of the person who you are providing care for and you will see a whole world of possibilities for visiting. This is hard to do but the more successful you are at it, the easier visiting becomes.

They can't hear me!

First of all turn down or off any distractions in the room (i.e TV or radio). Remember to ask permission before doing this. Would you like it if someone walked into the room and turned off your show? If there is a lot of noise in the hallway and it is possible to close the door then do so. If they are in a room with a lot of people, consider moving to another area of the room or another room altogether. In short, minimize the background noise as much as possible.

If the person is suddenly deaf since your last visit and you know they wear a hearing aid, you could inquire if they have it in and/or if the batteries are working. Sometimes this is enough to cue them to fix the problem themselves, otherwise you can engage the help of nursing staff or the personal support workers to help if you have the time. Remember that for people who use hearing aids annunciating words and being careful not to drop your volume at the end of sentences may go a long way in assisting the person to hear you.

Shout louder!!! All kidding aside, put your mouth close to their best ear (they usually lean it towards you or point to it) and talk as loudly as you need to, in order to be heard. Otherwise talking to you is like listening to the TV with the volume turned off. If that fails and the resident is able to read, write down (usually in very large print) what you are trying to say. It also helps to use any hand gestures that you can. I usually do hand gestures to keep in practice. For instance, any time I say a number under ten, I also indicate it with my fingers. Any way that you can point or act out what you are trying to say, all the better. Do not give up too easily on communication. That only adds to the frustration. Yes, you will look a little odd doing all this but remember that you are communicating the love of God...isn't that worth shouting about?

They can't see me!

For people who can't see, it is important that you not sneak up on them and startle them. We've all had that experience and the rush of adrenaline and wildly beating heart is uncomfortable. Remember that just because they can't see doesn't necessarily mean they can't hear, which is often an unconscious assumption made by many. You don't need to speak slower or shout louder because they can't see you. Also, it is important to remember that people who are legally blind can still have some vision so you will discover the limits of their vision as you get to know them or you may find an appropriate time to ask. Perhaps if you print a meaningful verse or poem in 48 point-sized print, it will be readable to that person. How thoughtful to maximize their vision!

They have aphasia!

Aphasia is a processing problem. Patients know exactly what they want to say but are unable to get the words out of their mouth. How frustrating! The best way to help them is provide supportive conversation. Supportive conversation begins by communicating to them that we know they know what they are trying to say. This helps them to relax. Reassure them that you have time to wait for them.

Normally we would consider it rude to finish other people's sentences and fill in words but it can bring great relief for aphasics. Everyone can remember a moment when they were struggling to come up with a word. You could see the image in your mind. Everyone around you was trying to help you come up with the words. What relief when you finally got it! This is the reality for every word of every sentence for aphasics. All help is gratefully accepted.

One of the best things to carry with you is a marker and sheet of paper. In large print write the words, YES, NO and ? on a piece of paper. Now the trick is to ask questions that require a yes or no answer and work patiently towards what the patient wants to talk about. The "?" is to indicate to you that you have gone on a tangent that isn't what the patient wants to talk about. If you are going to be having ongoing conversations with patients, go to the internet and download some pictographs. Pictographs allow the patient to point to pictures to illustrate what they would like to say. This also gives you a chance to choose your conversation in advance. For instance, if you want to talk about funeral arrangements, then you might have pictographs of a casket or urn so the patient can indicate whether he wants burial or cremation; a picture of the church or funeral home to indicate where they want a service, a list of popular hymns or Bible passages to point to. Incidentally, many aphasics can sing. Speech and singing are processed in two different areas of the brain. Sometimes they can sing their answers!

They speak a different language!

I'll never forget one particular gentleman who came into long-term care who spoke only Italian. He was terribly upset and the family was doing their best to get him settled. No one on staff knew Italian but one smart personal support worker leaned over his chair and said the only two Italian words that he knew which was "vino" and "mafia." The room burst into laughter and the tension in the room quickly dissipated as the family explained that mafia was not actually an Italian word but one that was developed by the North American media. His efforts showed how people appreciate all efforts to communicate and build bridges to them. Learning a few words can go a long way to reaching out and showing that we care. Finding and bringing books, music, pictures and cultural reminders can open up a lot of discussion. Finding people within our communities who speak the language can be really important. If you don't know someone from that language group, what an opportunity to meet someone! What a great chance to invite a family member to join you for the visit to translate so that you can get to know them too.

One of the most wonderful things about working in long-term care is the ability to see the full strata of a family. While the occasional church may see only three generations of a family, I often have the privilege of meeting five or six generations and many branches of a very large family tree that spreads across the world. Because the resident, generally speaking, isn't able to travel everyone comes to them. Furthermore, chances are the resident is in the facility they are in because at least one and usually many more family members are in the immediate vicinity. Many of them attended churches as children, were baptised, married, attended youth groups and other programs. Why not visit them when they are visiting their loved one and extend your care to them as well.

Wheelchair Etiquette

While some people in wheelchairs are paraplegic or quadriplegic, many are not. Even those who are, still have a wide variety of abilities. What difference does it make? Many people in wheelchairs are still able to walk, ambulate and move around and it is important that we not take away any of these abilities prematurely and not diminish their self-esteem by doing more for them than they are asking for. We may feel they are moving too slow but we need to bless them for moving at all.

You should never move a wheelchair without asking permission, telling them where you are going, the direction you are going and why you are going. Remember of course, that many people suffer from visual and auditory impairments as well so you may need to be in front of them and close to them.

Never lift patients or residents for any reason. If they need to be transferred from bed to wheelchair or vice-versa, use the call buttons to notify staff or ask staff. Workplace safety legislation does not permit staff to lift residents without the safety of mechanical lifts. To ask them to do otherwise it to put them a physical risk of injury and financial risk of losing their jobs. If you wish to take a resident somewhere, you need to arrive in time to allow for resident to be ready or even consider calling ahead and letting them know that you are coming for a visit and would like to take them outside for a walk. If you are leaving the property, you will need to have the permission of the power of attorney or family member if the resident is not capable so make sure that you have obtained that permission in advance. Be sure to sign the resident off of the floor or home area.

For hospital, the patients are not allowed to leave the grounds unless they have a doctor's order but can leave the floor with the permission of the staff for a change of scenery. On psychiatry and other locked units, some patients are restricted for their own safety from leaving the floor. Be careful not to promise an outside visit that you can't fulfill. If you would like to remove the patient to a chapel or outdoor space, it is best to try and obtain permission from staff away from the patient.

When walking with a wheelchair, do not move too quickly and take care to ensure that their hands are not on the wheels and their feet are lifted up or on footrests. If you are going a long distance, you may want to put the footrests on as it can be painful if the person you are wheeling suddenly becomes tired and drops their legs potentially jamming their feet into the floor. If you are going down inclines and ramps, go down backwards and when you come to a stop, make sure that you put the brakes on unless the resident asks you not to because they wheel themselves around.

Never make a person or a resident guess your name or ask them if they remember you? Remember how it felt when you met someone while you were running your errands and you just couldn't remember their name when they approached you. Remember how uncomfortable you felt and how your mind raced to try and place them. That is the experience of many patients and residents. It is better to introduce yourself and the church that you are representing as soon as you enter the room. Having a large print name badge is even better. Do not ask them if they can remember and give them clues as if visiting is some form of Jeopardy. On the other hand, if the person you are visiting does remember your name and other details it's nice to affirm that they remember.

They Don't Answer Me

First of all give them extra time to answer. Try this experiment. Ask the question, "How are you?" Wait a full minute and then ask it again and wait another full minute. You will be shocked at the number of people who will answer. They often need more time to formulate their responses.

Break down your inquiries into more simple questions. For instance, if I was offering you a beverage, I might ask you, "What would you like to drink. I have cold and hot drinks." You might respond by saying that you'd like a coffee and then I'd ask what you take in it (based on the assumption that you would remember the complexities of milk, cream, sugar, honey and sweetener). The same offering to someone with cognitive issues might look like this:

Would you like a hot or a cold drink?

They choose a hot drink.

Would you like tea or coffee?

They answer coffee.

Would you like milk in your coffee?

They answer yes or no.

Would you like sugar in your coffee?

They answer yes or no.

If they are still struggling, you could show them the milk and sugar and ask them to point to what they would like.

Whatever you do, do not fail to ask them, to give them the choice no matter how many times they have never given you an answer. Never walk by them without acknowledging their presence. Far too often we rob them of many things before the disease gets them.

They are Aggressive

Do not place yourself in harm's way. Be sure not to wear clothing, lanyards or jewellery that they can get hold of and cause you injury. If it is safe to remain in the room (leaving an escape route to the door) try remaining calm and talk quietly. Ensure that you are not within striking distance. Stand in a posture that is approximately a 30 degree angle to them with your hands down and palms open towards them. Unless there is a safety issue, do not argue with them. If you know them and know what they like to talk about, try to distract them with conversation. I have a tall resident who can get very out of sorts with his co-residents. The best distractions is for the very short chaplain to get alongside of him and ask him if he "gets wet first when it rains." He responds, "yes, but you will drown first." He then stands up tall and calls me "shortie" and he has forgotten about what was distressing him as he moves alongside me to tease me.

Often people are aggressive for a reason. Discover what the reason is and the aggression often disappears. Are they cold, hungry, frightened, bored, seeing things, afraid that they are forgotten? For patients suffering from mental illness and dementia, offering the opportunity for a conversation may help to calm them down. It is surprising how many people who have been trashing a room moments earlier will stop if someone will listen to them. We do not have to agree that their demands or requests are feasible or rational but listening can have a powerful effect on people.

When responding to aggressive people, do not make promises that you cannot keep or will put them or those around them in harm's way. Promising a cup of coffee can be something hot they throw or pour on themselves and many psychiatric medications and illnesses do not mix well with caffeine or alcohol. Remember that grape juice for communion may be more appropriate in some circumstances.

They Are Confused

Sometimes those who we are visiting are confused. They may have us mixed up with someone else, not understand where they are or what the date and time are. They may be operating under all kinds of false assumptions. My recommendation is to offer the correct information only once unless there is a safety issue. If the person believes that it is a good idea to run out in traffic, you must always correct (and preferably prevent) that choice. If they believe that it is Tuesday and it is really Wednesday, there is no point spending an entire conversation correcting that person. If they tell you they had tea with the Queen this week, do find out how that was. If they believe that someone is trying to kill them, then their fear is leaving them spiritually struggling so you need to reassure them.

Sometimes they aren't as confused as we assume they are. One resident complained for months that people were robbing her. As it turns out, those in charge of her finances were misusing her money. Did she know at some level that it was happening? Another resident told me he spent the weekend petting the Alpacas and Zebras. I went along with his story. A day later, the recreation team posted pictures of the residents petting the animals from the travelling zoo, which included Alpacas and Zebras!

Sometimes we must bring the resident bad news, such as a death or loss. The resident may grieve and then go back to asking for the person. Many people mean well when they keep telling the resident the news over and over again but since it is new information every time, the overwhelming grief hits them like a tidal wave. Every person is owed the dignity of being told once. If it is possible to take them to funerals or to see loved ones, then you may wish to consider this. Beyond that, constantly bringing up the information again is bordering on being cruel. It goes back to putting yourself in that person's place. Think of how you would feel if someone told you that someone you love has died. What if you couldn't remember and they told you every day for months.

At the same time, do your best not to lie to them. Remember that confusion is not always permanent and if they do come back to their senses and remember you lying to them, they may resent it or feel that you were making fun of them. Do your best to answer the questions without lying. If the person's spouse has passed away and they are looking for them and you don't want to put them through the grief again, you can simply say, "He's not here." Then redirect the conversation elsewhere. This is being truthful without being cruel.

Chapter 9

Prayers and Readings

One of the things that promotes the most anxiety for people providing spiritual care and visiting is prayer. The first thing I tell people is that you don't have to pray. In fact, if we are to pray ceaselessly, then we never stop praying and the choice is do we pray out loud. If we do, then a one sentence prayer is a prayer! "Dear God. Please be with Mr. Smith in hospital today. Amen." If you do wish to venture with more confidence into this area there are several things that you can do to gain confidence.

First of all, pray out loud in your own prayer time. Volunteer to pray out loud in less challenging circumstances such as grace or volunteer to lead prayers at worship or other gatherings. To begin with, you may wish to write out your prayer to read and gradually work down from something that is fully written out to bullet point and finally off the top of your head.

Mr. Smith is an 81 year-old man who was admitted to hospital after a fall. He had previously been living at home alone with a few hours of help each week with housekeeping. His son lives across the country and is worried about whether or not he'll be able to manage on his own or even if his father will be able to return home. During the course of the conversation, he talked about the many things that he is missing, including his cat and his garden.

When you think about this situation there are many overwhelming factors. The loss of health, the impending loss of independence, perhaps his home. His son is probably also overwhelmed wanting to care for his dad but living so far away will have his own responsibilities as well. The loss of a pet is overwhelming to many people as is the loss of activities that they love. Including a sentence or two about some of the concerns that you have heard says that the person was listened to and not only by you but by God.

Here's the important thing to remember. It doesn't matter how flowery your words are or how long you pray, God doesn't care and he doesn't send you a report card. For the person or people in the room who hear your prayer, it is most meaningful if it captures something of what they have shared with you. If you heard them and are reflecting that in the words of your prayer, then it provides assurance that God also heard them. For many people in times of crisis, the sense that God is present and in communion with them can be lost in the overwhelming emotions that accompany illness and the concurrent fatigue, financial stress, additional burdens of caring, fear of the unknown as well as the chaos.

The other meaningful way to pray is to recite scripture together such as the Psalms or to recite prayers that are well known such as The Lord's Prayer or the Rosary. For the dementia population some of the childhood prayers are meaningful. "Now I lay me down to sleep." (Although I personally never found it particularly comforting to consider the fact that I might die before I awaken and that something might be taken from me) nevertheless it remains a well known prayer.

If you are going to use prayers out of a book or from a traditional service, make sure that the words are appropriate for the situation. I have watched many infant baptisms of children who were imminently dying and the clergy read the same response questions that they would have asked in a church setting where the child was expected to live and grow up. "Do you promise to love and raise the child in a Christ-centred home" is a painful question to parents expecting to take their child to a funeral home for burial. With a few moments of thought, the question could be changed to reflect their reality to "Do you promise to love the child for however moments or hours that you have?" Reminding the family that as they hold their grief in their arms that One who is greater weeps with them. If you are called upon to do prayers, a service, a sacrament that is last minute, it is OK to ask for a moment to step out and arrange your thoughts and think for a few minutes what Scriptures are appropriate and what questions are sensitive to the situation. The exception to this would be patients that are headed for emergency surgery or transportation. In these cases, a short prayer with the patient present is all that is needed. Sitting for a longer prayer after the patient has been moved may be welcomed by the family but they also may just need some quiet space and time to sit quietly.

A Final Word

Spiritual care and visitation is one of the most important things that you can do in the life of your community. Illness, life transitions, trauma and tragedies take people by surprise and they may be unprepared for them. But the care that the community offers to them during these difficult times can be transformative and help them navigate the circumstances.

Following a response to these types of situations it is important that you plan some time to do some self-care. You must assume that you have been traumatized as well. You are one of the few people who will hear the story in all of its gruesome details. You are the one person that will see the entire story. One of the things that I do when I am on-call is check the newspaper to see what they reported. All details have been changed but I remember one day I was called to attend to a multi-vehicle car accident. The line the following day said, "Police were called to the site of a multi-vehicle car accident where a passenger died. Two victims were taken to area hospitals."

The reality of that scene was that there were two carloads of victims. One a young family with small children. The mother and father of the first vehicle were airlifted to the trauma centre while one child went to the local hospital and the second to the children's trauma centre. In the second carload grandma and grandpa had just picked up their children and grandchildren for a night of celebration on the town. They had just moved back into town and the grandparents were delighted that they would get to spend more time with their two young grandchildren in the back seat and the third one on the way. When grandfather made a left hand turn, he didn't see the oncoming car. It T-boned their car. Now I had six adults in the trauma room. The son passed away as blood spilled onto the floor as fast as they were trying to pour it into him. The baby was delivered and died. The grandfather, predisposed to heart condition was in such agony that he suffered a heart attack and passed away in the ICU. In the meantime, the remaining parents of both cars cried out to find out what had become of their children throughout the various emergency rooms. Almost 18 hours later when I left the hospital, I was emotionally and physically drained.

So why am I telling you this? The average person in the church will have no idea how horrific it is to attend to families in such distress. You must take the lead in caring for yourself. They read your week the same way the newspaper reads your week, in one single prayer request line in the bulletin. Because of confidentiality, you can't tell them how your week has been so you need to be firm in your own self-care and create your own opportunities to debrief, reflect, heal, nourish, renew, uplift, educate and repair your spirit, self-esteem, body, soul and mind.

If I have one passion in life, it is to see members of faith communities caring for one another throughout their lives. It is my hope that this book will have encouraged you to enter into this adventure, knowing that it will bring strength and resiliency to your community and encourage spiritual growth.

CPSIA information can be obtained at www.ICGtesting.com
Printed in the USA
LVOW06s1006090214

372940LV00001B/18/P